SPRING JOURNAL

Jonathan Gibbs is the author of two novels (*Randall, or The Painted Grape*, Galley Beggar, 2014, and *The Large Door*, Boiler House, 2019). His short stories have been anthologised in *Best British Short Stories* 2014 and 2015, and he curates the online short-story recommendation project *A Personal Anthology*. He teaches Creative Writing at City, University of London.

'Jonathan Gibbs has done an extraordinary thing with his response to *Autumn Journal*. He has created a restless, questing, witty, urgent piece of journalist-poetry (to use MacNeice's own phrase), so particularly of the surreal and helter-skelter times we've recently lived through it seems both to chronicle and to make sense of them in real time.' – Lucy Caldwell, author of *Multitudes*

'It's a triumph. I'll be buying copies for all my friends because this is going to be my bible and companion in the dark months to come. Line after line sings with truth.' – Linda Grant, author of *When I Lived in Modern Times* and *A Stranger City*

JONATHAN GIBBS

Spring Journal

after Louis MacNeice

 editions

First published in 2020
by CB editions
146 Percy Road London W12 9QL
www.cbeditions.com

The author and publisher acknowledge the support
of the Estate of Louis MacNeice, author of *Autumn Journal*,
© 1939 The Estate of Louis MacNeice, published by Faber & Faber

Printed in England by Blissetts, London W3 8DH

ISBN 978–1–909585–37–9

To David and Michael
and to my grandmother Jo

NOTE

On the evening of Thursday, 19th March 2020, I had the idea of tweeting about the coronavirus epidemic in short poetic bursts, inspired by Louis MacNeice's long poem *Autumn Journal*, which he wrote in late 1938 in response to the impending world war and described as 'not strictly a journal but giving the tenor of my emotional experiences during that period. It is about everything which from firsthand experience I consider important.'

I created a new Twitter account, @SpringJournal, and wrote two tweets that evening, and six more the following day, each tweet containing four lines of poetry in MacNeice's 'elastic kind of quatrain'. By the end of March I had written a little over 40 tweets, the equivalent of two of MacNeice's 'cantos'. Around this time David Collard asked if I would be interested in having *Spring Journal* feature in a series of online salons he was organising during lockdown called 'A Leap in the Dark', where they would be read by novelist and actor Michael Hughes (like MacNeice, Michael is from Northern Ireland).

Michael read the first two Cantos on Friday, 4th April, and from that point onwards I wrote a canto a week, sending it to Michael and David to be read out on the Friday evening. I took MacNeice's poem as a loose model: sometimes working out from specific lines, sometimes engaging more broadly with the themes of individual cantos, sometimes ignoring the original as I responded to world events. The final canto was performed as part of a complete readthrough of the whole poem on a special 'Leap in the Dark' on Friday, 28th August, with Michael joined by guest readers, and original music composed and performed by Helen Ottaway and Melanie Pappenheim.

J.G.

October 2020

I

Close and slow, spring is starting in London,
  Creeping up through thickset lawns that though too wet to cut
Still taunt the retired asset managers and accountants
  Who would be out there by now for certain but
Strange thoughts stay their hands from the Barbour
  On the hook in the hall, and the lead and poop-bags by the door,
For this spring brings headlines from Italy and China,
  And nobody knows what anyone's allowed to do any more.
And it's March coming in as the last daffs are fading,
  And the first nasturtiums coming, blithely ignorant of the farce,
And the mother popping out to Tesco despite her daughter's anguished
                                                    warnings,
  Raising her eyes to the few remaining planes that pass
Westwards from Heathrow, which is no longer owed an extra runway.
  For so it is we learn to live in air that's good to breathe,
And the canals in Venice running clear, with little fishes swimming
  And the tourists at the airport asking when they'll get to leave.
And it's Friday night in London where the pubs are all still open
  For the blessed who think it's fine to drink then loll home in an Uber.
Do they raise a glass to those still stuck onboard the MS *Braemar*
  Turned away from every port till they were taken in by Cuba?
And all the worries, social anxiety and taxes,
  And whether Stella will marry and what to do with Dick
And the great-uncle who lost his savings to a doorstep fraudster,
  And is this tightness in the chest merely asthmatic?
And the growth of vulgarity, electric scooters on the pavement
  And the rising tide of plastic on the beach
And the hiking LGBTQ+ lovers with thoughts directed

Not to God nor Sovereign Nation but each to each.
And the queue for Sainsbury's this morning was a sight to behold;
  The shoppers with their trolleys
Running right around the car park – 'At ten to seven! On a Saturday!' –
  Are just the highest tide mark of our ongoing infinite follies.
So I'm Tweeting this from the till queue trailing up aisle 27
  (Where there's plenty of shampoo and hair spray)
And there's eggs and bread and bleach and chips and lasagne,
  But even those might be gone by now I dare say.
And the question of privilege raises its head,
  As of course it does,
In every aspect of the current situation,
  And what each one of us does
And can possibly do is permanently affected:
  The tins I'll decant
Into the food-bank dump bin by the exit
  Are, let's face it, scant
Atonement for my middle-class security,
  And the gofundme
Donations for artists and writers
  Faced with shock redundancy.
So let's hear it for Picturehouse cinemas, sacking
  Staff as a matter of course,
And for the Coylumbridge Hotel in Aviemore,
  Which 'apologised for any upset caused'
After laying off a dozen workers in what it called
  An 'administrative error',
God knows what goes through these people's heads as they write these
                                                              letters,
  If they understand the terror.
The terror? Is it terror? This fluctuating fear, anxiety and worry
  All laid one over the other like card laid over card,
And everyone I speak to seems broadly fine, but there are others
  Online that this crisis is hitting more squarely and hard.

And I am in the car now and the sun is out as we are heading east
   Bound for the Essex coast, and the shuck of wave on shingle,
The visit to my wife's parents, to deliver essential items and offer solace
   But not to hug or kiss or even mingle.
And we sit in our parked cars and eat fish and chips from cardboard boxes
   Watching the too many people on the esplanade, and the not-enough sky,
For we cannot eat in the flat, and the communal room is closed,
   And this is the English way.
And the drive back, yawning, with the sun low in the windscreen,
   Though it's now that it gives its most singular light,
Painting the winter wheat a rich green-gold and dotting
   The turned brown clay with Canaletto white.
And as I stand pissing against the hedge, I notice the first hawthorn blossoms,
   Simple specks in a complex pattern,
Like you'd find printed lattice-wise on wallpaper,
   Or on a cushion or curtain.
And so back to London, with its own uncertainties evolving:
   The density of people, the space and air we share,
Where the warm spring wind blows us dangerously together
   And infects our complexes and cares.

Written 19 March to early April

II

In the back garden the newly hatched bees
    Act out their strange low-intensity frenzy.
How odd that it puts the human heart at ease,
    The sight of this feeble, frantic, unceasing passage
From blossom to blossom, barely stopping to guzzle at each.
    Is this not pleasurable? Is there no joy to be taken?
You are bees! Those are flowers! Can you not teach
    Us to be more like you, or less like ourselves?
We who were up like good Christians to Lauds
    To try and get our online orders in
Ahead of the hordes –
    You are number eighty-three thousand, six hundred
And forty-seven in the queue!
    And as dawn breaks into the bedroom the screen is something
That seems to come between the world and you.
    The screen exists outside of time,
It does not come into leaf,
    Like something almost being said
Its open tabs do not relax and spread,
    Nothing in them is like a kind of grief,
The screen cares not for your sleep, the ache in your flesh;
    Its only trick, the only thing it seems to say,
Is that you must refresh, refresh, refresh.
    Yet while the shops are still open we'll go and collect
Our respectably ordered books,
    Though even this exchange comes limned with distrust,
And grim swift sideways looks.
    And this too is hard: parked up in Eastbourne, becalmed,

In view of the sea;

The horizon splitting the windscreen high in my eye-line,
The sky a pale blank, blue and serene,

And I'm on a mission to deliver to my ninety-year-old grandmother
A Google Nexus 7,

So she can see as well as hear the family who cannot
Care for her now, cannot hug her even,

So I come armed with disposable gloves of rubber
And anti-bacterial wipes,

Ready to log in to next door's WiFi, then teach her
The touches, the presses and swipes

That are second nature to us, but that she has long laughed off,
'I should have got on that train when I had time,'

She said, when pressed, but now we're forcing her on,
Though the steps be hard to climb,

And I must do it at two metres distance, or from another room,
And quickly, and in gloves,

And knowing that my very breath, my touch,
Might infect that which I love.

And on the drive down I listened to Backlisted on MacNeice
And his *Autumn Journal*,

And one thing that was said struck me in particular:
'It's good when poetry is useful.'

So yes, MacNeice is useful. He shows how the political
And the personal are closely knit

Yet distinguishable, and how to be a philosopher and a 'sensuous man'
And make the two things fit.

And on the A22 the trees thicken their branches against the sky,
And on the heath the gorse

Is an untrammelled explosion, caught and held just so,
And in Paris the Bourse

And in London the Stock Exchange plummet and rally
And plummet again,

And we must hope this engine we've built

Can stand the excess strain,
    And that the falling castle which has never fallen
Will be standing when all this is done
    Or that what remains of the castle can be reused
To build a new and a better one.
    We need to learn to count, and to learn what counts,
We need to learn to move beyond the quid pro quo,
    We need the lesson of the bees in the garden – which perhaps
Even the frantically flower-fucking bees don't know –
    That there are more flowers than bees in the garden.

Written 23 March to early April

III

March is nearly over, the people
    Back not from holiday, but from planned
Work trips, are relieved to be home. There is no joie de vivre,
    None at all. It is absolutely banned.
Then it's back to the working week, with a non-ergonomic
    Desk chair, email, and Zoom.
And the tidied shelves behind where you sit in your office-
    Cum-bedroom-or-living room,
And the student's lecture in bed that they're somehow all the same late for,
    And the pupil's virtual lesson,
And the Catholic sinner's suddenly authorised
    Straight-to-the-Big-Man confession,
And the poolhalls standing empty, the squash courts, saunas and lidos,
    And the barbers and bowling alleys,
And the beauty parlours, the nail salons and wine bars,
    And the chapels in the valleys,
Which means where are all the people? They are at home, of course,
    And the main distinction now
Is not between the jobless and those with jobs
    But in whether or not you have to leave the house.
And another distinction: not the skilled vs unskilled workers
    Of last year's vicious points-based system
But the starker split between essential and inessential workers,
    And therein lies true 'social distance'.
The distance now is between those who hold society together, ventilate it,
    Underpin and help it grow,
And those who harvest its pollen, siphon off profits
    To lay down like last year's Bordeaux.

And we live in an inside-and-outside world, our doorstep
Is a kind of Rubicon
Crossed only to fetch in the carefully set-down deliveries
Or for our daily walk or run.
Let the doorstep be a place of communication!
Let us stand there and clap!
Let us look up and down the road and see where
Our lives converge, connect and overlap!
And the garden centres ditching thousands of plants unplanted
And the fruit that will rot on the bough
And the bankers forgoing their annual bonus
And the goats running wild in Llandudno town,
And we know the government has acted, but that thousands
Of small businesses will go to the wall,
Which leads one to ask, what are jobs, businesses and bankers,
What are governments even for?
What will there be when we emerge from this crisis
And its developing adversities?
Will there still be theatres, cinemas, bookshops, galleries?
Will there still be universities?
Will the standard of intellectual and cultural living find its level?
For though it's easy to say
There will be singing about the dark times, the singers
Need somewhere to play.
And morning brings birdsong in the garden,
And the gleam of frost on the lawn –
The silence this spring is that of the traffic
That we used to hear in our sleep, that ushered in the dawn –
And the rising death toll on the radio, for the strange tenor
Of this new crisis is the fact
Of its invisibility; it cannot be seen from the window,
Or on the TV, its only point of contact
Is in posts and reposts on Facebook and Twitter
To say that somebody's loved one has died,

And we count the steps that join us to that person
And so it spreads through our lives.
There are no corpses in the streets, no body bags, no visible sign
That might help to diminish
The disconnect of the fact that right now, in Britain, someone dies
Every two-and-a-half minutes,
And when this is all over, how easy it will be to forget what it was like,
For it was like nothing at all, a weightless dream,
It's the nurses and doctors who'll be like soldiers back from the trenches,
Unable to talk of what they have seen,
For we wouldn't believe them if they did try to tell us, we'd be too busy
Turning our face to the wall
Or trying out our brand-new get-up
For the upcoming governor's ball
And April is upon us now, and most of us are still to find out
If we will rise to the challenge it holds, or become unstuck,
We who have been lucky so far, but cannot be sure if we've laid up
Enough time, and luck.

Written 30 March to 2 April

IV

April has come and I wake
  But I cannot think with joy of the future,
For something there is abroad that can take
  That future away; it does so in silence,
And it's coming closer, not yet in my street,
  But in my timeline:
The retweet of the desolate tweet
  That a partner, a parent, a cousin has died.
And if MacNeice wonders
  Whether 'the conditions of love will be changed' and 'affection not lapse
                                    to narrow possessiveness'
Then as for me I'm under
  No illusion regarding that particular manoeuvre.
And yes, alright, Louis: April has come, it is hers,
  Whose blood lifts a notch in the springtime,
But whose nature prefers
  The more rigorous glories of summer,
The pure straight hit of sun and heat,
  Not for the leaves stunned to life on the branches
But for the joy of sandals on feet
  And sunglasses tangled in hair,
And so I give her this month and the next . . . and the next . . .
  Though they are likely to be ours regardless,
As we face the new and strange context,
  She with even temper and hopes, and projects, even.
So I am glad
  That my life is circumscribed by hers, with her ambitions
Reaching farther than any I can claim I've had,

Who is more ready to rhyme beauty with duty;
Whose mind is like a shuttle on a loom
Weaving threads the rest of us don't notice,
Whose eyes glint like irony in the gloom,
Whose laugh is a fieldful of birds taking all at once to the heavens.
To whom I send my thanks
That our life as it unfolds offers unexpected vistas ahead and behind,
And if there are blanks
Then those are there for us to fill together,
Not alone,
Walking a beach that seems to roll from Scotland to Cornwall to Essex
And as we walk we'll stop and count each unnumbered stone
Slipping only the most superb – the most stony – into our pockets.
And perhaps it was easier for MacNeice
To make Canto IV of *Autumn Journal* a love poem,
For his subject was not there to police
His words – and you are. So here goes:
Frivolous, when you feel like it, early for every flight,
Frowning only at your own thoughts, taking particular notice
Of trainers and handbags, for your work wardrobe is tight-
ly constrained: a carousel of cardigans rich in competence and style,
Rarely untidy, if we ignore the loading of the dishwasher, often elegant,
Wearing your first grey hairs like a newly awarded degree,
On occasion too easily hurt, though never arrogant,
With your love that can need provoking, which is itself provoking,
For long-term love is a form of knowledge that comes mixed
With not-knowing,
And how those elements are arrayed is not fixed,
And is itself unknowable, which is part of the pleasure.
Who won't talk about films you've seen, or books you've read,
Who presses her feet sole-flat
Against mine to gather warmth in bed.
But now to last night's news, that our prime minister
Lies in intensive care,

Which makes a neat thought experiment for anyone who hates his party
And him in particular: does he deserve our 'thoughts and prayers'?

No, not especially. We can hope he doesn't die
And still wish he wasn't in charge at this of all times,

There are others more deserving of our sympathy,
The families of the bus drivers who have died – now nine.

They, like him, deserved better leadership than was on offer,
And the doctors and nurses dead or very ill,

Or still working twelve-hour shifts, sixty-hour weeks,
With missing protective equipment. Mere good will

Is not enough for them; does he want some of it also?
And tonight the full moon fills the street, and no sound

But a Chopin *Nocturne* sifting faintly from the speakers,
No clapping for Boris, but all around

The silence of houses folding in on themselves for the night.
And you, unloading the dishwasher as I write; I can hear the clink

Of cups and knock of cupboard doors.
This house will fold around us, and I think,

I hope, we'll live in it until it kicks us out.

Written 3–7 April

V

Easter weekend was beautiful, the sky a warm considerate
　　Blue, the best for weeks and weeks,
And though there were egg hunts in the gardens there were no
　　Family visits, no trips or excursions; our techniques
For living have turned inwards, now we try our hand
　　At sourdough starters, high-impact online workouts
And improvised obstacle courses,
　　And all this activity is aimed at drowning out the fears and doubts,
For the question on everyone's tongue is:
　　Will life ever be the same again?
Or no: not everyone's tongue, because for some life is already
　　No longer the same: it is utterly changed,
My sourdough starter
　　Is your food bank voucher. My obstacle course
Is your daily navigation round a violent and abusive partner.
　　Life will not change itself; it will only change through force.
And in the park for my morning run the cherry blossoms
　　Cheer me on, pink as pompoms, and the parakeets,
And the posters telling us to keep our distance
　　And on the radio Trump speaks, Trump speaks
From the Rose Garden, and if you can bear his voice you'll hear
　　The US has pulled its funding for the WHO,
And there are forest fires closing in on Chernobyl
　　And lava spewing out from Krakatoa.
And if this seems like proof that nature continues despite the virus
　　Then let that be a corrective
To the videos of goats in Llandudno, and boars in Barcelona.
　　Nature's operations are not so interconnected

That wildfires will stop, and floods cease, just because we happen
    To have other plates to juggle, other issues to arrange.
The drop in air pollution is a blip; we have not flattened
    The curve of global climate change.
And we laugh it off and meet for Zoom drinks in the evening
    And this, we say, is on me:
Something out of the usual, a new local craft ale –
    But did you see
The latest? You mean whether Dylan's dropped another new track
    Or that old lad's hundred laps on his zimmer frame
Or d'you mean so-and-so's face-mask post on Instagram –
    No, we don't mean anything like that again.
What we mean is Covid, Contact Tracing, CFR,
    Self-Quarantine,
The panic that cramps the lungs and twists
    The spine into the spleen.
And when we wake in the morning and reach for our phones
    The feeds are the same as the day before,
And we compare national data sets, and we compare the graphs,
    And for all this information we cannot be sure
What it all means for us; as individuals we are used to choice,
    But the choice here is no game-changer:
The choice is simply to stay at home or, for those who must,
    Go out to work, and ever-present, grossly unintelligible danger.
The newspapers and websites are racing to deliver what news there is,
    And hoping to get paid,
And the Bank has extended the government's overdraft
    And you and I are afraid.
And perhaps fatigue has set in, as they said it would. For what can we do?
    We cannot march in the streets, as for Brexit, and Iraq,
We can email our MP, clap the NHS,
    And go for our daily run in the park.
But people are burning down telephone masts, while politicians
    Repeat their dull refrain on PPE,

And the bloody, bloodless frontier is endlessly converging
    But never arriving; the future state of the economy
Is a problem for better minds than ours,
    We only ask that the old order be overturned
And things remade in a fairer, nobler fashion, and this new more thoughtful
                                                                    way of living

    Be maintained – and also that the things I've earned
Stay mine. It is no good saying
    'Take away this cup, bring me a new cup, with a handle and a spout';
Having helped to fill it up ourselves it is hardly
    Just that we should simply get to throw it out.
And we can hide our heads in the sand, Louis, for there is always
    More sand, cascading down,
And it's no good relying on the cooing pigeon for a sure critique
    Of the values of the town.
The bins are being collected, the milk delivered,
    And yet the crystal ball remains opaque,
And if we're sleeping through the world's dream of its own death and rebirth,
    Then today is not the day when we wake.

                                    Written 15–18 April

VI

And I remember Spain
   In summertime, ripe as a mango on the point of liquefaction,
Our holiday was a home exchange:
   One terraced London house for one flat in suburban Seville,
But with a communal pool,
   And air conditioning, for which no perfect setting existed,
And the boys learning Spanish at school
   Had the writing on the wall and the menus to read.
With cheap beer in tumblers,
   With café con hielo over great lunks of ice,
With plates piled high with prawns in La Mar de Gambas,
   With the walls of the Alcázar
Jealously hoarding its shadows,
   And its floors rilled with ribbons of water,
And its gardens augustly disposed
   For slow hot walks under oleander and jacaranda.
And the cathedral courtyard's orange trees
   In rows, though the inside reeked of glitz and gilt,
And the saints' bones in their reliquaries
   Except where absent 'for liturgical purposes'.
And the bat we found
   In the Parque de María Luisa,
Lying helpless on the ground,
   And that we placed back in the shrubbery,
But carefully, lifting it slowly with sticks;
   That bat the only portent of the coming disaster.
There were no other signs, no simple tricks
   For avoiding what has now landed squarely on us and squashed us flat.

Yes, the standard of living was low,

    But that, we thought to ourselves, was not our business;

What the tourist wants is the status quo

    On a plate, at half the price, in a little place

Not even TripAdvisor knows about.

    And to be a tourist today seems not anachronistic but obscene.

Last month we were still holding out

    For this summer's holiday, already booked – not now.

Now we wonder

    If we will ever see the Alhambra, Baixa, Rialto,

If we will have the gall to wander

    Those ranked and storied streets gloved and masked;

That's what being a tourist is:

    Walking other people's streets uninvited and unasked.

Those 'sights' are hers, are his,

    Not ours; those cafes, restaurants and bars,

If they ever take their shutters down,

    Are for them to sit and eat and talk in, not for us.

This crisis has thrown

    The old ideas into abeyance,

And the new ideas are as yet

    Untested: indistinct and inchoate,

They are the lens through which our grandchildren contemplate

    Our lives with vast, appalled regret.

Frequent flights, a pound of meat

    On every plate; people housed like animals,

Animals crammed into concrete

    Silos, and all of it hidden, from thought and vision.

And so I feel the pull

    Of something I can't quite fix down, for maybe this isn't

Princely asceticism after all,

    But puritanism, base and resentful, that sits back and ponders

As the economy teeters on the precipice,

    And I work on my jigsaw

Of *Las Meninas*

Bought in homage at the Prado,

And only finished now

We have time on our hands – and our hands, which need keeping

Busy any old how,

Sift through the shreds and shrapnel of 'the true philosophy of art'.

So I remember Spain,

Not as a premonition of the current state of affairs

But as a quivering membrane,

A portal into a time no one wants to say is gone.

And the next day we flew

Home, not realising

That Spain would become be a fortnight-ahead preview

Of our own incoming fiasco, our disaster;

So look to Spain, Italy, Germany, and compare

The policies, the testing, the excess mortality numbers,

And then measure and compass and plumb your despair.

Countries will have to learn how to look at each other again.

Written 18–23 April

VII

Video conferences, postponements, missed targets,
    Daily briefings, castles in the air,
The autopsy of letters by senior civil servants retracting previous statements,
    The protracted death of laissez-faire.
Or as the English call it, just Keep Calm
    And Carry On,
And let the corporations carry on ruling the roost
    And treating like so much carrion
The lives of those whose exertions oil the machine –
    It's not our labour that they need,
Nor the goods produced by that labour, but our consumption;
    Our wants and lacks are there to feed
Their balance sheet, but with US crude dipping
    To minus forty dollars a barrel
The world economy seems like something lifted
    From the books and mind of Lewis Carroll.
And as the weather turns, the rain comes misting
    The air with veils of grey,
And as with the rain, so for the national conscience,
    Which is thankful not to have to face the brightness of the day.
Today, good weather is bad news, it lures us out
    Into a world we are no longer
Free to enjoy.
    The urge for freedom in some is stronger
Than the need for safety; would it not be better
    To hibernate till this is over?
Sedate the body politic, ventilate it, and give it precious
    Time to recover?

And the talk is as much of exit strategies

    As of where we currently are,

But exit into what? Do we owe the world our patronage, is the world

    Just one tremendous bazaar

For us to spend in? Greece wants its tourists back

    To get the Greek wheel turning,

With the implication that it's our personal duty to ensure

    Our neighbour's annual earnings.

And if here there's a graph showing projected deaths and there one showing

    Projected GDP

Then plenty of people's eyes are shifting between them,

    Seeing only what they want to see.

So think of a number, double it, triple it, square it,

    Emblazon it across the sky.

Now tell me what it was that you were counting

    And can you look that number in the eye.

And across the ocean Trump's press conferences have turned brief

    As if he too at last is sick of lies.

We don't believe a thing we hear; the very idea of belief

    No longer applies.

And they are taping up the outdoor gym in Mayow Park

    So it looks like something out of *CSI*.

All this talk of the Blitz lifts no one up; there are no bombs,

    The searchlights do not probe the skies for bacilli.

We need to turn the searchlights on ourselves

    And on the mechanics of the state.

'Now is not the time to ask what went wrong';

    No, let's leave it till it's far too late.

For time, everyone agrees, has lost its agency,

    It explodes, extends, collapses on repeat,

We're not living in the new normal yet, but in the terrible interregnum

    When the numbers expired on the balance sheet

And more people died than the government

    Cared to admit,

The government fumbled the ball. The government
  Was frit.
And the rivers are not teeming with corpses, though the
  Corpses must be piling up somewhere,
And hospitals built in a week stand empty
  And the only excess stock is in despair.
And so when I woke this morning to my forty-eighth birthday,
  My first thought
Was not that I was happy, but rather I was *thankful* to be alive.
  And the juggernaut
That came and ran us down still has us under
  Its eighteen wheels,
It will carry us with it for miles and miles, and into
  Next week, heedless of our appeals.
And I ran around the park again this morning,
  So I am tired,
And the post came at last, and the sun came out,
  And still no one I know has died.

Written 27–30 April

VIII

Sun shines easy, sun shines gay
   On shuttered bookshop, cakeshop, market,
On lido, casino and penny arcade,
   On Trafalgar Square and its sleeping lions,
On the gastro pubs and the tapas bars,
   On the pavement queues and the pavement traffic,
With the glance to the eyes and the masks and scarves
   Pulled tight across the nose and kisser.
Half my life I've lived in this city,
   Working my way around a way around words
In newspaper offices, a small university,
   Teaching ways around words to a gaggle of students;
Hemingway, Chekhov, Woolf, the usual round,
   The passive voice and the run-on sentence,
And to hear a new poem read aloud
   In Monday's class: 'I really like what you're doing.'
But life was comfortable, life was fine
   With a partner, family and career,
And all of this learned, from sine to cosine,
   In the calculus novus of the self in the world.
The croissants were fresh, the parties were fun,
   The walls were painted in Farrow and Ball,
Things were done, undone or half-done,
   And nobody cared, for the days were young.
Nobody niggled, nobody cared,
   The soul was cocooned by the interest rates
That were, and remain, historically low; the soul was unprepared,
   But the television flickered on the walls and ceiling.

And we drove around Kent in an MPV –

    Margate, Whitstable, Dungeness, Hastings –

Yelling along to 'Echo Beach',

    'Gimme Sympathy' and 'Helter Skelter'.

And sun shone thinly, sun shone dense

    On cherry tree and raspberry bushes,

And foxes lolloping over the fence

    With raddled tails and eyes of augury.

We slept in Egyptian cotton, we cooked with Spanish wine,

    We transferred the balance and paid no mind

To how the sum of debt inclined

    And hummed, with the hum of background radiation.

We were safe outside the dotcom bubble,

    Were married three days before 9/11,

Bought a flat, then a house, with minimal trouble,

    Lost nothing in the crash but our sense of balance,

And have salaried jobs to keep us afloat:

    It's the generation behind us

Who missed their spot on the boat,

    Or were pushed out, rather, as the boat left the harbour

And the harbour was mined and set to blow;

    Let them sift through the debris of a future

That we mortgaged and held in escrow –

    They've time enough to reckon their zero-hour losses.

But roads ran easy, roads ran gay,

    As we followed an atlas clear of the city

For a well-earned, well-heeled weekend break

    West to Bath or the Brecon Beacons,

And diesel, which praise God was cleaner than clean,

    Was less than a pound to the litre,

And the speeding car unrolled the endless green

    Of England's rental rural history.

But that was then and now is now,

    The car stands idle at the kerb,

The country's for the country, the town for the town,

   The brow of that hill, the dip and curve of that valley,
The tranquil shade of that bluebell wood

   Is a memory held close under the tent of the bedsheet,
And the sun, like a thing only half understood,

   Pricks the air in places, which grows purple, and fades.
And the crisis hangs before us

   Like the flipside of a memory,
And the stage resounds with the lamentation of the chorus:

   'The right steps at the right time, guided
By the best scientific advice'; yet here we are

   With 32,000 dead, and more not counted,
And more to come. No matter how low you set the bar

   We have not reached it, we're barely adjacent.
And we curl up on the sofa for the National Theatre Live

   The soaring *Twelfth Night*, the dismal *Frankenstein*,
And we welcome new babies for Boris and Carrie, and Elon and Grimes,

   And wave to the asteroid as it passes.
And once again

   The crisis is denied, with lies piled on lies;
Our press is four fifths rank, its stain

   Will not wash out with mere tears and shouting.
And here we are – just as before – safe in our skins;

   Glory to God for VE Day
Put out the bunting and bang on your pans,

   Call it winning, then go down fighting.

                                        Written 3–7 May

IX

'Now we are back to normal, now the mind is
   Back to the even tenor of the usual day
Skidding no longer across the uneasy camber
   Of the nightmare way.
We are safe though others have crashed the railings
   Over the river ravine; their wheel-tracks carve the bank
But after the event all we can do is argue
   And count the widening ripples where they sank.'
So run the first eight lines of Canto Nine of
   MacNeice's *Autumn Journal*,
And I cannot improve on its sense or sentiment
   Except to say that we are *not* yet back to normal,
The camber of the road ahead is uncertain –
   The road itself is in doubt –
And we'll not be done for years with counting the ripples
   And watching them widening out.
May bank holiday weekend comes, with the filthy *Sun*
   Tempting us into the light
And filling the streets with parties (the London parks
   Are a dreadful sight).
And this week my work turns from teaching to marking:
   Parade, in close order, left/right dress,
With me as drill sergeant of creative writing
   Inspecting recruits for proof they possess
Originality of thought, style and form,
   Boots polished, creases sharp, stance symmetrical and neat,
Understanding of generic conventions,
   Double-space your work, indent, repeat.

Never use a metaphor, simile, or figure of speech

    You are used to seeing in print.

Don't tell me the moon is shining, sunshine;

    Show me the glint

Of light on broken glass (break the glass if need be).

    Be her on whom nothing is lost;

Give me the vivid continuous dream, the five-act structure, give me

    The seven basic plots.

And here's the axe for the frozen sea within you,

    Which in your case you have not got,

And here's the splinter of ice in your heart,

    Which is always released, is it not,

With an easy flick of the finger, and please do not let me see

    Anyone using his thumb,

Now here's a bill for nine thousand pounds, here's a reading list,

    And turn to chapter one.

But can you *teach* someone to write?

    Of course you can't, but perhaps you can *learn*;

Teachers are those who stand and point the way

    And now and then discern

The spark of talent that merits kindling;

    I'm not here to train

The next platoon of Rooneys and Heaneys,

    I'm here to tend to their brains:

Their critical thinking, the habits of mind that

    Hone the intellect,

That make for clear analysis and elegant expression,

    And when these things all intersect

Then maybe you'll have an education,

    And maybe you'll know how to write,

But more to the point what you write'll be worth reading.

    And maybe then you'll join the fight.

For we are governed by Humanities graduates – mostly –

    Who seem determined to throw

Our subjects under the bus of 'employability'

    With all the glory, all of the dough

Funnelled straight to STEM subjects; which, don't get me wrong,

    Would be fine

If when science was needed they didn't ignore it

    For some desperate Nudge Unit line.

And I want to tell my students: the world needs you, because it needs people

    Who know how to think

And how to analyse that thought and express it

    In words that don't make you blink

And say, am I reading that right? Stay alert, Control

    The Virus, Save lives?

Whether you're a student of Rhetoric, or of Comms,

    That's not one for the archives.

And MacNeice had his Greeks, all so unimaginably different

    And all so long ago

But our subject is right outside, so I say to my students,

    Yes, write what you know,

And if you're good enough, you'll soon work out

    You know next to nothing at all

About what you thought you knew. That's when you start digging,

    That's when you answer the call.

And the crooks are still out in the Agora, the careless athletes

    And the fancy boys,

And the slaves, libation pourers, and demagogues, they're all still there,

                                  listen:

    Listen to their noise.

Written 9–15 May

X

And work this year will see no cap and gown
  In the back rooms of Westminster Cathedral,
No procession up the nave, no celebration lunch in town
  And garden party back on campus.
And I think of the ends of other terms,
  Other marquees in other university grounds,
And memory reaffirms

  The thrill and exhilaration of ending something well
And among friends, who you know you'll leave behind
  As you push on into life; these are they with whom
You'll reconnect, if time is kind,

  And look back at how what you achieved together
Set the tone
  For what you would achieve apart from each other,
And you pose in variant groups, for camera or phone,

  For exhilaration is the grandparent of nostalgia.
It's odd these moments should claim
  Our attention; they were not when we were most alive,
But when we paused life to give it a name.

  Life is something in the background,
Expressing itself in textures and scents:
  A television on somewhere else in the building,
A table where you worked, a creosoted fence,

  A tally as vast and arbitrary as our 25,000 genes,
Each one waiting for its cup of tea and madeleine,
  Its apotheosis in a glance or a hiccup,
Or the half-heard refrain

  Of a pop song trailing from a passing car's window.

But we tossed our caps and raised a glass,
    Half-drunk on expectation of the future.
That prosecco must taste flat to the class
    Of 2020. The door opens for them onto a wasteland,
No jobs, no prospects; the economy is scarred
    As the buzzword has it, but what caused the scarring,
And why weren't we better prepared?
    A stab-proof vest, not miracle gels, would have been preferred.
They won't take it for granted that things
    Will get bigger and better and better and bigger,
They won't expect to pull on the strings
    To have cushy days roll in from over the horizon.
While for me school – a grammar school in Essex –
    Did provide a fertile bed for growth, though not only
As defined by the dominant metrics
    Of exam results and future earnings.
We ran comedy shows on the school hall stage
    And formed ramshackle bands in the prefab huts left over
From a simpler, humbler, beiger age;
    We covered them with murals, and now they're gone.
So there are no junior ministers or captains of industry
    In my year's notable alumni
But musicians from the main stage at Glastonbury
    And comedians from off of the TV.
We didn't get to go on the dole,
    But we did get to make schooling a frolic
And a revel – though maybe the whole
    Thing's the same big sentimental trick
Each generation gets to play
    On itself, and these kids will look back at their education
With the same self-serving whimsy, and say:
    We were so *young*, and the days were golden.
And today is the warmest day
    Since last August; the sky belongs to the cloudlets

And the few contrails of planes
      That passed earlier unheard; and this morning
The birdsong seemed to come not just
      From the gardens close by, but round them,
Through airways clear of smog and dust,
      From all the birds of Forest Hill and Sydenham.
And I think of the Year Sixes,
      Who may not get their last weeks of primary school –
For, yes, ending something well carries riches
      Not all of which get reinvested in what comes next.
And though the schools may still open
      In June, in spite of the concerns and cares,
The bond of trust has been damaged, if not broken,
      For all education is built on trust, then love,
And only then on grammar and spelling,
      And the basic numeracy of what R equals today.
Tomorrow there's no telling
      What children will bring home with their homework.
And the summer looms like a bright black hole,
      As infections decrease and we lift our heads and wonder
If we understand the next part of the role
      We're being asked to play in this terrible opera.

Written 17–21 May

XI

Midway upon the journey of our life together
    We found ourselves in a wide bright clearing.
There was no way of knowing which way to turn,
    The path kept appearing then disappearing,
First on one side, then on the other.
    The sun beat down; the space seemed to extend
Forever; there was no way onward, we thought,
    No route by which to descend
Safely to civilisation. The hike was not aborted,
    But on hold,
We sat on our cagoules and opened our rucksacks,
    We'd supplies enough, and at least it wasn't cold
Or raining, as on other hikes, or hailing,
    Or blowing a gale.
This spring is that clearing; we must be patient
    And sit tight till better conditions prevail.
And while MacNeice heard the sound of his lost love's voice
    As if through a wall
Of indifference and abstraction,
    I hear yours through the door down the hall.
And it's true we know each other's voices
    In all their moods and modes.
Your voice on the phone, to the cat, to the children,
    Our voices when we speak in code,
Exploring new pathways into a quarrel,
    Taking turns at who goes first:
'I'm not your student!' 'Well, I'm not your patient!'
    Our lines are very well rehearsed,

For any married couple worth their salt can argue
    About anything at all
If they put their minds to it; love loves nothing like
    The grimly paradoxical.
But listen, Louis: a tempestuous two-year affair will make a very different

                                                                                    poem

    Than a marriage of twenty-odd years,
The joy and anguish even out, to leave behind something
    Beyond either kisses or tears.
But here, in this bright clearing, it's getting hard to tell apart
    The world and us.
We are and are not a mirror the one of the other;
    We cannot simply frame it thus
And say: the world is gone awry, but we are all right;
    Perhaps we aren't.
Perhaps the sickness of the world only shows and heightens
    The sickness in our heart.
And we were out in the world today; it has become a faded image:
    Picnic spots turned to meadow,
Shops boarded up, the great prairie-sized advertising
    Hoardings tattered and yellow.
Soon they will be renewed and refreshed, when people
    Are sure we'll buy
Whatever trinkets they have to sell us: throw open the doors!
    Unleash the supply
Of bread and circuses – put your togas back on.
    For this is Roman weather once again,
Though in this circus of death the bloodied victims are
    Nowhere to be seen,
They are away in makeshift morgues in hangars and factories,
    Neatly out of sight,
When they should pile up in our every thought, their shadows should
    Block out the light.
And war had its photographers, skilled at framing evil

For the weekly magazines;
There are no such remembrancers for our tens of thousand dead.
Instead on our screens
We see a familiar menagerie of liars and dissemblers
Blocking the path ahead.
First of these is a leopard: we know him well, he's always changing his spots,
He weaves in place and bobs his head.
Then, behind him, his boss, a cowardly lion,
Though for all that
Ravenous indeed, careless in his appetites, rotten in his thinking,
Contemptuous of caveat.
The last, a male she-wolf, gaunt and wayward and depraved,
And the most dangerous of the three,
He hungers for destruction, with a hunger that goes unsated,
The wolf he scares me, Louis.
He makes me long for a guide, as Dante had a guide,
Who will lead us up the hill
To truth, though of course *his* route to Heaven
Began by going down to Hell.
And Louis, if he appeared before me now, would say, 'Jonathan,
There is no Heaven, you know this,
And if there were I could not guide you. I was no good husband or lover,
As I'm sure you noticed.
Noticing, not guiding, is what I did. That she-wolf,
Who has poisoned your already poisoned spring,
That's good. Keep doing that.' And he goes, and we sit, the two of us,
And look at each other, in this wide bright clearing.

Written 25–29 May

XII

These days are gorgeous, preposterous, bright,
   The sunniest spring since 1929,
But with no rain to speak of for weeks
   The garden would be in sharp decline
Without close attention and water and care.
   And without care and attention democracy withers,
The death of George Floyd is proof, for those that need proof,
   That racism is still and always with us.
The lunatic demagogue has got white cops
   Thinking they've the right to murder
Unarmed black men;
   This is the death of law and order,
And America is on fire again.
   Its White House skulks in the shadow,
While outside a church stands the devil, with a Bible,
   But the Bible is hollow.
And peaceful protestors in thousands are met
   With tear gas and rubber bullets,
And the Lincoln Memorial is lined with troops,
   Badgeless and faceless in face masks and helmets.
And here, too, the government won't tell us
   How many black and brown people have died from the virus,
It would be in bad taste, they say;
   There is no worse taste than conscious bias.
Racism infects all the parts of the body,
   It reaches the eye, the tip of the finger
That types the words into the screen
   That confirm the belief that black lives matter.

And we lean further and further into our screens,

    But each screen is a mirror;

It shouts back what we know to be right,

    It compounds every error.

And when we wept last week for our thousands of dead

    We were scared only for the future,

But the world is never slow to show us our worst face,

    Our stupidest expression, our stupor.

And the crowds are at the beaches,

    And the golfers on the fairway,

And thanks to the nation's resolve, horse racing

    Is back from Monday.

And the House of Commons, too, is open

    Once again for voting,

If MPs will only line up in the sun for hours

    And don't mind promoting

A system that tramples their own best interests

    And of the people they're there to speak up for.

Democracy fails in a million ways,

    You don't need a jumped-up dictator,

You don't need people coughing, screaming, crying,

    You don't need forcible denial of liberty.

It can be enough to join some stupid ritual dance

    Out of a previous century,

Or to just not see the neck under your knee,

    And your country's colonial history,

And reading Proust on his plans for his book,

    I bury myself in a sensory

Oubliette; some people long for a shroud,

    Or a weighted blanket,

I lose myself in this involuted tract on aesthetic creation

    And think it a banquet.

Now it is morning again, the 4th of June,

    And there has been a shift in the weather,

Outside it has forgotten how to rain;

    The streets hunker under the pressure.

And Proust is wrong; just now there is no past, no *in*

    For involuntary memory,

We are stuck becalmed in a hellish present. This is Thursday

    The 4th of June, 2020.

And I move from Proust to Baldwin, because what can you do?

    You need somebody to learn you,

You need to think that the books on your shelves

    Will help when it's them that you turn to.

'Any real change implies the breakup of the world

    As one has always known it, the loss

Of all that gave one an identity, the end of safety.'

    That's Baldwin, here's MacNeice:

'All I would like to be is a human, having a share

    In a civilised, articulate and well-adjusted

Community where the mind is given its due

    But the body is not distrusted.'

But, Louis, the body is brittle, and the mind is a trick,

    And you don't get to live in

That kind of community just by raising your hand,

    Reality's not that forgiving.

And we should stay indoors, but the streets are telling us to

    Get out and move on from clapping.

So turn off your screen, get up from your chair,

    Open the door and let the night air in.

Written 2–5 June

XIII

Which things being so . . . but then that's the problem:
    For the things that last week seemed 'so'
Are not so today; the world changes seldom
    And when it does it changes slow,
And last week was anger and pain and confusion
    As the bad old news from before
Broke into the strange new nowhere we're living in
    And pushed our face to the floor.
And we said hey, we've got heads full of graphs and back-to-school schedules,
    Give us time to take stock,
But they went right ahead and tore down a statue and rolled it
    Into the dock,
And after Colston, Rhodes and Leopold, and a dozen other statues
    To vicious, powerful men,
Are gone or lining up to go, and shitty little *Little Britain*'s gone, and
    Should have been gone way back when,
And Minneapolis stands up and shrugs and says it can function
    Just fine without the police,
And our mouths drop open, and the words don't come, for when they shouted
    No justice, no peace
We missed that the answer was there all along: justice
    Comes *from* peace. Let people live
Without fear of the knee on the neck or the battering ram;
    Let people conceive
Their own systems of care and support,
    Give them power to arrange
The struts and levers and cogs of their world, but my god!
    So much has to change!

For systems are not statues, to be torn down in moments
    And rolled in the street.
A system like this is a house of many mansions,
    And not all of them en suite.
And while I can say I didn't help build the house that I live in
    You could say I inherited it,
Or I inherited my room, which is on quite a nice floor, with quite a nice view,
    And no one likes a hypocrite.
For this is the change of the last week: from looking
    Out to looking in
And being looked *at*: not where do you stand on this or that
    But where does your work begin?
Stop tweeting your support and signing petitions
    And sewing your heart on your sleeve.
What will happen next in the world will not happen
    Just on the strength of what you believe.
And if intersectionality has a lesson
    It's not simply that we've got to learn
To see in ourselves our constituent elements,
    But how to be seen in turn,
And accept that the circles we draw – so carefully – around ourselves
    Might be all one from where you sit,
That from there it looks like I'm in the same circle
    As plenty of people I think are just shit.
It's going to be hard fucking work, long hours and hard labour,
    You can't do it in a poem.
You do it in your place of work, in your town, your village,
    Anywhere that the system
Benefits you, where the system's your ally;
    It's not about proclaiming whose back you've got,
It's about looking behind you to see who's got your back
    Whether you like it or not.
So yes, white privilege has got my back, and racism
    Has got my back too,

And will go into bat for me each time I walk down the street
　　Or into an interview room.
And thank god for the streets, because the world online
　　Appals like an open wound,
And when the discourse turns hateful it's hard to balance
　　The need for quiet with the need to be good.
And it's open the schools, don't open the schools, open
　　The zoos instead,
Who can you fuck, can you go the pub, does your two-metre
　　Bubble begin in your head?
And we want this to be over, so we can start pushing the boulder
　　Back up the hill to the top,
For Colston, the bastard, is back on his plinth, and needs rolling
　　Each day back into the dock.
So tell me where to stand, and sorry you have to tell me,
　　But this shit is never going to stop.
Hold me to my expectations, call me out when I'm weak, and most of all
　　Tell me when to shut up.

Written 8–11 June

XIV

The next day we drove – by day –

    On roads again crammed with cars and lorries and motorbikes and scooters,
All full of an insane sense of themselves, like a spray

    Of roadside flowers revived by a long-awaited downpour,
Out on the A12 and the A133

    Past Thorpe-le-Soken and Kirby Cross,
The odd St George's flag hanging limply,

    The odd roadside stall with plants for sale and an honesty box,
That mix of amour propre and the need for outward show

    That says, this is England, we stand for what we believe in,
And if we don't precisely know

    The meaning of our beliefs, well belief is a kind of feeling
Better understood in the gut

    Than the brain, as much inchoate as incoherent:
England land of piers and painted beach huts!

    Nowhere more than seventy miles from the ocean!
And at the beach the tide was in

    With only a few families still splashing and playing,
And we stood with the waves slapping our shins,

    And let the dirt of the North Sea cleanse us,
And while we stood there like so many useless Canutes

    'Statue defenders' were pouring into
Trafalgar Square to make Nazi salutes

    And attack the police – and remind us that football
Has been away for months, and that overweight, balding, violent thugs

    Are as much part of the national picture
As monuments to murderers and commemorative mugs.

    And we sat on the greensward at Frinton

And drank lemonade and ate cod and chips
    And watched a kestrel carefully hovering over
The bluff, and move on and hover again, and the light was rich
    And the people were gone, and an hour of early evening
Early summer sun
    Is like a foretaste of eternity; smack your lips and
You can taste it on your tongue,
    Salt and sweet like a can of pop drunk within reach of the breakers.
And three days later I sat on a bed
    At St Thomas', by the river,
And I watched the nurse unbag the needle and spread
    Its green plastic wings, a mechanical mosquito,
Proboscis prepped for my vein,
    And he tapped my arm and leaned and pressed and
In it went, no hint of pain;
    And as if by magic the snaking tube was sleek with the claret
Of my blood, and on went the vacuum
    Tube and I watched it fill, slowly,
The red of my life and the quiet hum of the room,
    As if all of this was something entirely ordinary,
And it was hard not to see the world
    As made up of primary colours, like a picture book or a nursery poster.
The serenity of it was absurd:
    Yellow sharps bin, green scrubs, red foolscap folder
With my obs and my consent,
    While I watched my life being deftly extracted,
And only then the main event:
    The vaccine – or not the vaccine, this being a blind trial –
In its own splendid syringe
    Presented for injection in my opposite shoulder
And in the moment just before the plunge
    I saw the liquid in the barrel was transparent
As if there was nothing whatsoever there,
    As invisible as the virus, begging you not to believe in it,

To see conspiracy only in the air,

   Then just the itch in the skin to say something had happened.

And the room where I went to wait

   For another nurse to check me over

Looked right out at the river, at the great

   South Bank Lion of County Hall, the London Eye, the tourist boats at anchor,

And she, like everyone I'd spoken to

   Except the receptionist and Matt the curly-haired doctor,

Had a foreign accent; we owe so much to

   People who come here to save us from ourselves.

And I cycled home through Burgess Park

   Where people stood on tiptoe to pick cherries

From the trees along the cycle path,

   And then down the Camberwell Basin canal, that we walked up

On Millennium Eve,

   And there was more of the week to come: Union Jack planes, Marcus

                                Rashford,

The rainy return of the Premier League,

   But for the moment leave me here, on my borrowed bike, legs turning,

                                arm throbbing.

Written 15–18 June

XV

Stormzy and dubstep and TikTok and Tinder
    And day returns too soon;
We'll get plastered at the free bar
    In the revamped catacombs,
Give me an aphrodisiac, give me a swipe right,
    Give me the same again;
Make all the erotic poets of Shoreditch and Streatham
    And Peckham and Brixton and Penge
Lend their honied bars to my wicked purpose,
    And let us give the DJ thanks
For the warp of the bass and the strobe of the sequins;
    Let the old muse get out of her Spanx,
Or give me a new muse, in something from La Perla,
    Hair waving like a flag,
With mascara as black as the cosmos, fingernails of crimson,
    Dressed by Valentino, with a Chanel clutch bag.
Let the gamers run riot round Fortnite Island,
    Let the graphic cards all glitch,
Flip your gender in Faceapp and see if you fancy
    Yourself as a himbo or bitch.
Give us distractions, and again distractions –
    Deep fakes, fireworks, vagina candles, bling,
Spend your bitcoin, spunk your PayPal,
    Let the critical thinking go out and the Twitter pile-ons begin.
Give me a fuckboy, but fuckboys are too easy,
    Give me a saint,
We'll feed him to the trolls, smear him across the meme pool
    We won't countenance complaint.

Bring on the Insta-girls and the influencers,

    Let them bow to our conceit,

Bring on the stans and the also-rans,

    The end of all this shit will be so sweet.

But look who comes here. I cannot see their faces,

    Walking slowly, slowly, one by one;

They're coming from the hospitals and care homes,

    Their faces are pale in the late June sun,

Or see-through even. I wonder where they're going,

    Could it be to the golf club,

Or the model village, bingo hall or theme park,

    Or just to the pub?

Each has an oxygen mask around their neck. I wonder

    Who let them all come back?

Who signed their discharge papers, snipped off their wristbands?

    Is someone somewhere keeping track?

And they're four-deep at the bar, and knocking at my elbow,

    When there should surely be no trace

Of any of them anywhere; they should be gone, or invisible.

    There is something familiar about this one's face.

And this one, and this one also,

    Where have I seen them before?

They're crowding the public houses,

    And those that can't get in are banging at the door.

But take no notice; pass the menu,

    A drink to start would be nice,

The English must have their pub, it's their mother's milk,

    So a bottle of fizz, some beers, and a double G&T with ice and a slice.

So how've you been? Tell me about it! Look, don't stop talking,

    And yes please show me that highly amusing thing on your phone,

And show me another, and another, and maybe those horrible vacant

    People with blank faces will give up and go home.

Just pretend they're not there, you've had plenty of practice,

    You've been in training since you were small,

And when you look again they'll have vanished,

    What do you mean, they haven't vanished at all?

This is getting beyond a joke; I didn't come here for trouble,

    And don't get me wrong,

But they would have died anyway is all I'm saying,

    So pass me the mike and give us a song.

'Try Not to Breathe' by R.E.M., or the Police doing

    'Don't Stand so Close to Me'.

What this whole country needs is a proper sesh and a nosh-up,

    A kebab, a Morley's, a Maccy D.

Come on lads, it's my round, what you having?

    Don't let yourself get put off your stride,

Those aren't people standing silently at your elbow,

    Don't act like somebody died.

So why do you hold your hands over your eyes like that,

    And shake your head in quiet despair?

Pull yourself together, come on mate, why won't you answer?

    I can't answer because they are still there.

Written 20–25 June

XVI

Nightmare leaves fatigue:
 We envy men and women of action
Who sleep and wake, murder and intrigue
 Without being doubtful, without being haunted.
But not today. Today doubt is a mark of worth
 (The best, as we know, lack all conviction)
And insomnia a badge of truth:
 Who sleeps well, wakes under a cloud of suspicion.
And I wake a suspect English man,
 I suspect my thoughts, and my own reflection,
And I dare myself to see if I can
 Unpick this inheritance, as MacNeice unpicked his Irishness.
Like a schoolboy writing his address
 As *England, Earth, the Solar System,*
The Milky Way, the Universe, so here are the names I can profess:
 I'm English, British, European –
Well, *British* seems a busted flush,
 The English don't care for their neighbours,
Who by and large want rid of us,
 And are edging away in thought and action,
And seem ready and willing to make the leap.
 So let devolution lead to secession,
Let the children of Empire weep
 For the ashes of their statues and stature.
European is the greater loss:
 The ties were there from childhood, threaded in a daisy-
Chain of summers, the journey across
 The Channel, by ferry, then tunnel,

To camp in Brittany, the Loire, or the Cévennes,
    To wander the aisles of the hypermarchés
For Danette, Kiri, brioche, madeleines,
    And the 'chore' of cycling for croissants in the morning,
And the warm breath of the lunchtime baguette,
    As miraculous as Easter; France was an object lesson
In showing how sophisticated simple things can get.
    And from this, all of Europe was a logical unfolding:
Paris, Berlin, Copenhagen, Seville,
    Sartre, Beauvoir, Bernhard and Jansson,
Marías, Ferrante, Gainsbourg, Brel;
    The whole of the blessèd European canon
Was a window onto a widening present, a deepening past
    And a future of plausible splendour,
But a future we could not make last.
    Which leaves *English*,
The least part of myself, because the part least known,
    Who'd be English anyway? An island history
Fit only for infants, a nursery rhyme, a tarnished crown,
    Bad teeth, worse manners, a platoon of old maids cycling
To Holy Communion through the mists
    Of Orwell's autumn morning,
But the church stands empty, that Soho pub no longer exists.
    What remains are the queues for the Labour Exchanges,
And the lorries on the Great North Road
    Piling through the pissing rain for their next-day delivery –
No, when I think of the English I think of the English abroad:
    Fish and chips on the Costa Blanca,
Crapulousness in the hot Med sun.
    What the world must think of us – for what we show them,
Now, in 2020, let alone for what we've done
    In the past. And that sense of fair play? A vicious empty slogan.
The best we can do is point and say,
    Look at Orbán, Putin, Erdogan.

We're not as bad as China or the USA!

   Let veils hang over the mirrors,

Let the history textbooks blanch to white,

   Let the litter on the beaches

Mark the place we said we'd stand and fight.

   And let me choose English as the hill I'll die on,

Not as a birth right, but as a spot upon the soul;

   In the time of the fading of nations

Where you're from is a shrinking part of the whole,

   A badge on the lapel, a flower in the greater garden,

So let England shrivel – or let England wake,

   Not as Arthur from under the mountain,

To do press-ups until the enemy quakes,

   And not as a butterfly, something newly divine and precious,

But simply as a statement of intent,

   To be what we always said we were, but never questioned,

To read our own small print,

   To speak softly, and listen, and make a bonfire of all big sticks.

Written 29 June to 3 July

XVII

Sitting having breakfast at the kitchen table
    We see the clouds process the busy sky.
The leaves on the branches agitate in sequence – on the roses
    In the garden and the sycamores nearby,
And breakfast today is the Keto diet:
    Avocado, two poached eggs, no slice of toast,
For the fact is that under lockdown
    My self-control has largely given up the ghost.
Not enough exercise, too much bad food eaten standing in the kitchen.
    The inner life dissolves as the outside world expands,
The sofa's an abyss that beckons nightly,
    And lotus fruit comes weekly, boxed, in vans.
And yet this calamity could still cure us
    Of the need to go out and congregate and fuel
Our ritual self-serving exchanges
    With cataracts of alcohol and unsubstantial food.
No more nights of shouting over each other's shouting
    To establish who for this particular moment is right.
If man is a social animal, then consumer culture
    Is its perfectly adapted parasite.
And if the pubs and restaurants go under, what about the theatres
    And galleries and concert halls?
Will we all stay home and mutter nostrums
    For the benefit of our four bare walls?
And lying in the bath, the theatre and the concert hall are phantasms,
    Protective scaffolds for the soul,
The ego must subsist on what it alone can furnish;
    And a dog with another dog may be more whole

Than a single lion, Louis, or a dog trotting
   By itself, but in the end we're all solitary dogs,
The phenomenal world is sustained by the barks and
   Yapping of our endless private monologues.
And other people are there to fuss and plump the pillows
   Behind our weary head,
And stroke our hair and hold our hand and promise that something
   Will survive of us when we are dead.
And I lie in the bath and think of Plato
   And these are the thoughts that rise through the steam,
For the bath is the fount of all solipsism,
   A mini-break in a pop-up womb,
And these days you and I take baths together
   Less than we did in the past,
But one after the other, not to waste water,
   And for each of us to hold fast
To that moment of quiet in a hectic life, and a household
   Full of noise,
The world will be there tomorrow, there will be washing
   And feeding and chivvying the young men we still call boys.
And Plato was right to tell those people sitting
   In their cave to switch off their flickering TV set
– Or, as it might be, mobile or laptop –
   And go and do something less boring instead,
But on the other hand broad-chested Plato
   Was wrong to condemn
Our liking for gazing at shadows, for we often see things clearer
   When we're stood at one remove from them.
So don't make me look at the truth directly,
   Don't batter me with the absolute One,
Only mad dogs and philosophers
   Go out and stare at the midday sun.
And yes, summer is upon us, the longed-for
   Apex of the year,

We run with open arms to hold it
    Yet when we reach it, it is not there,
But half behind us;
    It holds the year in equipoise,
The opening out on one side, the gathering in on the other,
    We must not think of it as a warranted pause;
No, we should be looking to the future,
    Not curling in on ourselves;
Go out on the town with your government voucher
    And look at the menu, the goods on the shelves,
And don't ask why our spending's more vital than our earning
    Or why the economy depends
On us giving out more than we can gather back, ever,
    Or where the hard money stops when the sweet music ends.
Our decisions are bets on future success,
    Like banking on light from a faraway sun
But that star is so far from our poor solar system
    That when we get there I fear it will be gone.

Written 6–10 July

XVIII

In the days that were early the music came easy,
  On vinyl, cassette tape and compact disc,
Songs for the kids and songs for the grown-ups,
  Torch songs and slow jams and bangers and brisk
Bouncy ballads that severed your heartstrings
  And bounced their way straight to the top of the charts;
All the A&R men knew, what was good for the business
  Was good for the art.
And we howled when they said home-taping's killing music,
  But it's streaming that's doing the deed,
The artist held tight in the pure algorithmic
  Vice of the new technologies,
And then the slow extinction of the venues
  For the sake of the landlord's slice:
Regeneration – into what? We're sold back what was taken
  From us, as a memory only, at double the price.
Who'd be an artist?
  The system feeds you crumbs
Unless you give it a brand-new cake of your own invention,
  Or until ambition succumbs
And you adapt to crumbs as a permanent diet,
  Or you perish in the attempt;
Yes, there have always been penniless artists
  And the world has ignored them or shown them contempt.
What's different today is the cooing, flattering
  Grip of the universal vampire squid,
The Creative Industries will squeeze out their cut with cuddles
  And then have you say that you're happy they did.

The bedroom producer and self-published writer
    Know it's never been more easy to make
Anything; it's getting it heard that's harder,
    Smuggling it safe past the guard at the gate.
And with the screen the world is your market
    But not your oyster; it's hard to know how close
To shrink your focus, when billions of fans might be waiting
    To download the ditty you've just now composed.
And I think back to a summer on Ynys Enlli
    And the time we sat all evening long
In the schoolhouse for the Nosen Lawen
    With simple stories and jokes, music and song
On the harp, the guitar, the bagpipe and fiddle,
    Nothing compelled, all given for free,
The air calmed and coiled like a cat, the air moved inward;
    What passed around the attendees
Was the delicate yarn of communion, wound lightly,
    And nothing would leave the room
But the remembered fact of association,
    And the smoky end of a singular tune.
And likewise these words find their highest value
    When Michael reads them – right now – to you
And they pass through phone lines and cables
    To die on your ear drums: all their revenue
Is there. For art is fine, and having
    Money is nice,
And it's grand to be paid for doing something
    Well, but there's more to the price
Than what you earn from it. The world holds onto
    A part of you when you venture out into its craw,
And the more you give yourself up to its purchase
    The harder it is to withdraw.
And there is no hero in the artist,
    No genius to worship or honour or dread,

God made no artist when he made Adam,

And Adam cares not if God is dead;

It's commerce that makes the general weather

And rules the local waves,

If God's still living, He's god-damned useless,

And hiding no doubt in one of His caves,

Fearful as Adam of being discovered,

For the knowledge He ate in His apple was this:

He's created a monster, that's swallowed his creation,

And each thing it touches is for the abyss.

And art can't convert the devil, any more than it can stop infection

Or cure the tainted crops,

The crisis unfolds quicker than words can handle

And the queues now are outside the banks, not the shops.

Too many are dead, but jobs are dying too, all over.

The virus reveals the flaw

In our way of living: the rich fly it around the planet

And dump it on the doorsteps of the poor.

Art cannot undo this; at best, like Ariadne's

Thread, it can help you out of the labyrinth,

It can lift the beleaguered spirit,

Like it lifts a woman onto a plinth

And fixes her there, arm held up in salute,

And, yes the earlier days had their music,

But there is other music out there – right now – taking root,

If your ears are attuned to the coming acoustic.

Written 13–16 July

XIX

Parakeets slice the London air,
    The shutters stay down on the chain-store windows,
Colston's plinth stands void in its square
    Speaking for no one, speaking for no one.
Leicester's factory workers daren't stay home,
    The microwave pings and dinner is ready,
Some are hungry and others are gone,
    A smiling face in a Facebook tribute.
And faceless the Uyghurs in Xinjiang,
    Faceless the fascist police in Portland
Roaming the streets in unmarked vans,
    Faceless the troll farms and Russian hackers.
And faceless the nurses in masks and gowns,
    Faceless the firms with PPE contracts
Of hundreds of thousands or millions of pounds
    Got with no government tender or bidding.
Each day the world is more hard to digest,
    It shrinks and grows in a series of circles
That cross and diverge in a fearsome complex;
    The decree to think global, act local
Has never been so tough
    To follow. What is wrong with the planet
Seems blatant enough
    But what do to? How to act? Where to place your first footstep
When the guidance changes from day to day?
    And all will be normal by Christmas, no question,
So let the workers spring like a corps de ballet
    As they weave their ways down the busying pavement.

Dodging the streetsweepers pushing their carts
    Filled to the brim with our sins of omission,
Let the measure of intimate distances start,
    O what a busy morning!
Kids on bikes, trapping or trapped,
    And the office workers with nails of coral –
But lashes untinted and faces unwaxed,
    And small hope of heading anywhere foreign
This summer, and those on furlough face news
    Of their jobs and their futures fading to nothing;
The second wave will claim its dues,
    And December will tip as if without warning
Into a new disaster, a new pox, a new blight.
    If Covid is the wolf then Brexit is the vulture
That will pick on our corpse till the bones show white,
    And still there is no vaccine for political folly.
And here is where the poet turns his well-turned lines
    To the woman who'd left him alone and deserted –
The second in a row, poor Louis – yet still he can find
    The means to be kind: he embraces his freedom,
And wishes her luck,
    While for we two the hypnosis rolls on unabated,
The belief in the bargain we struck
    Two decades ago, to be true to each other,
Holds firm; the song that we sing has kept the same tune;
    Our job is to endlessly make up new verses – variations
On the theme of a long-gone honeymoon,
    When we are so long in love, are we even in it?
And god, Louis, you were thirty-two
    When you wrote *Autumn Journal*,
So young! You burned through
    Life like you were chain-smoking summers,
And of course I read your cantos
    As the work of a master, a mentor, a teacher,

The statesman in the photo
    With thinning hair and a stare like my father's.
But you couldn't, it seems, mix sex and art
    Successfully; like the blueprint for a cocktail
Overheard at a party, but what part
    Gin to what part absinthe would be always beyond you
When you tried to remake it. What makes some love affairs succeed
    While others fail and falter?
As well to say it's in the distant stars' decree
    As fix it down with human logic or earthly reasons.
But the booze can't have helped; those bright busy mornings
    You'd have seen through a blur
Of headache and regret – empty bottles
    And full ashtrays – but regret is a spur
To art, as poetry is carved from chaos:
    You cannot write what you cannot feel,
And it's one thing to wrestle with a blizzard of emotions
    And another to coast on an even keel
Through life. And you, my wife, did not sign up to be a muse,
    It was a prose writer you married,
Turning up in poems was not part of our vows.
    So I sketch these lines with tact and devotion,
And on this latest busy morning, my dear,
    As you cycle off to work I am glad that you are busy,
For busy mornings make survivable years,
    And I wish us luck and I pace myself, for the sake of the party.

Written 17–23 July

XX

Wind buffets the island of Thera,
    Nothing here that cannot be blown
And stay in place: collared doves and sparrows
    And some kind of kestrel, the sprinkler-fed lawn
And the flickering pool, complete with jacuzzi,
    And edged with bougainvillea and tooth-leaved palms.
Yes, we have fled into luxury,
    To pick grapes straight from the vines
And contemplate the view of the caldera,
    Sign of the disaster that destroyed
A culture from long before Plato,
    Long before Homer, Achilles or Troy.
The island blew itself into the sky
    And sent a wave rolling over to Knossos
That did for them, or set them up for the Mycenae
    To take them out when they descended.
And yet this other, older world persists
    In frescos and fragments,
Amphoras, ewers and pitchers: not gifts
    And treasures, but household items,
All buried under hundreds of feet of volcanic
    Rock and ash, and so preserved
For us to warm our hands on, thirty-five centuries later,
    So beautiful and so undeserved.
What is our work when set against this meagre archive?
    A film against a fresco, a poem against a pot?
What gets put into art is by no means equal
    To what gets taken back out.

And the use of a painted pot to its former owner

    Is different to its usefulness today,

It is and is not a memento mori:

    Not just reminding you that you must die

But that something of you will survive,

    And what that is, is not of your choosing:

Those ribbon-tied letters go in the recycling,

    The photos are wiped from the laptop hard drive.

Take all of this, and all our hard-won culture,

    Now throw it into the air

– Every million-seller, every prize-winner –

    What floats back down is posterity's share:

A few half-burned remnants,

    Some packaging, some scraps,

Curators of the future will put it back together wrongly,

    They'll skip over the lines and read into the gaps.

And we walked the empty ruins of Akrotiri,

    Peering down at the rooms and squares

That huddle and climb in the same haphazard

    Pattern as the town above ground whose stairs

And alleys we followed the previous evening,

    Google Maps in hand, in search of food.

You can only build in one manner

    On this kind of land – haphazardly; do we then conclude

That the people are the same today

    As then? That a Greek remains a Greek whether

Ancient or modern, that the clichés

    Now were clichés then and equally valid?

The sea is the same sea, and not the same sea,

    The way it stretches towards but does not meet the horizon;

The sky stealing down to mix with the Aegean

    And rob you of the sightline of eternity.

There is nothing wine-dark about it, nothing loud-roaring,

    The women here are not 'specially ox-eyed

Or the men high-hearted, as Homer and Henry Miller
    Have it, immense in their natural ability and their pride.
It is an island of scrub and cliffs and six hundred churches,
    Of roadside white-trunked trees,
The roads themselves full of dinked white Fiats and couples on quad bikes,
    The houses painted white by decree
Of the generals' junta, and now kept freshly
    Painted white for us.
We come here, as Americans do to Scotland,
    To pay our emotional taxes at our lost ancestral address.
It is a place to stare at the sea and sell yourself the lie
    That because we have managed
To make it this far, intact, if heavily damaged,
    Then the next three thousand years will fly
Equally easily by, and that anything the world can throw at us
    Or we can throw at it
Is of no account, that throwing pots or writing poems
    Is not ridiculous arrogant folly, not superfluous.

Written 28–30 July

XXI

As the war loomed in 1939, Henry Miller fled Paris for Greece,
  We don't need razor blades, he decided,
Or canned goods or lawyers or explosives,
  We just need solitude and idleness and peace.
We should pay no mind to the truth as dished up in the papers,
  But lie still in the sun for most of the day,
Letting the book-learning dribble away
  And not caring why people are killing each other
Elsewhere in the world. And though I have flown
  To the same light-consecrated country
I lack Miller's cocksure composure,
  And anyway the news is stacking up at home;
And giving up the news altogether
  Is just as bad as being transfixed
Or addicted, and since the messages are always mixed
  Our job as good citizens is to disentangle
And valorise the different elements
  Of hope and disaster, and to judge the proper dosage
For our welfare, such that the message
  Doesn't overwhelm and drown the sense:
The second wave is building,
  And this time it won't be in spring
With summer still a-coming in
  And a single school term to keep from collapsing;
This is summer, our blessed respite,
  And what is building over the horizon
Might not be a wave but an ocean
  As wide and dark as the night.

Now is the time to ask, not just can we counter

    A crisis (we can't), but can we plan?

Can we look deep into a less than

    Certain future and put down markers,

Can we quit the cycle of upbeat, knee-jerk replies

    To immediate problems

And admit that tomorrow

    Might be less happy and glowing than advertised?

And the sea as seen from the mountain

    Might be bright and noble and serene,

Might be a mirror where the mind can pose and preen

    And think that its thoughts are of infinite value,

But up close, from a boat, it is indeed as dark as wine

    And roaring, even when it seems most placid;

It is a thing very far from abstract,

    But not a thing the mind can mine

For meaning; it will swallow you and your meaning

    Whole, and not even spit you out,

It is no refuge or redoubt,

    Light does not penetrate far into its darkness.

Anthropomorphism is a weak defence

    Against the otherness of nature;

We look for human features

    In rock formations cast by geologic events

We can describe in a textbook but not fully

    Integrate when face to face

With a beauty and a seeming grace

    That would annihilate us in an instant.

And the cabin of the plane home is a hard straight

    Tunnel plunging you back to a present

That waits, like a tolerant parent,

    Ready to overlook the fact you are home so late,

Prepared to forgive, so long as you knuckle

    Down to your chores,

Tidy your bedroom, clean out the drawers

And make a good start on things in the morning.

But equally it seems unfair that the world

Hasn't managed to sort out its problems

While we were away, or in transit,

And left things wrapped up for us on our return

Like the post stacked neatly in the hallway,

The flowers watered, the cat fed,

And clean sheets on the bed,

Or that universal communism, like Christ, has not descended

And all are somehow equal under the sun

Without us having to lift a finger,

And the papers fold for there's no news to publish,

And we are blessed in spite of what we've done or have not done.

But no, there is England, lying pale and drawn outside the window,

Manifestly unchanged, unlovable and unable

To love, so we fasten our seatbelts, stow our tray tables,

And steel ourselves for our onwards journey.

Written 28–30 July

XXII

August the eighth: under low grey clouds
    The air blows fitfully and broils itself
And becomes unbearable; we cannot allow
    The summer to go on in this manner.
Wimbledon Common could be the Serengeti:
    What grass there is ground down to dust;
The trees survey the sere and yellow
    Veld, and flinch beneath the heated gusts
That would shrink each pond to a puddle,
    Each puddle to a square of dirt,
And as the sun drums down on the English Channel
    Scattered dinghies attempt a new Dunkirk:
Families from Iraq, Iran, Sudan,
    Crammed into their fear, risk the crossing from Calais
With or without the middleman,
    The peril of leaping always less than remaining.
And damn those who condemn as 'very bad and stupid
    And dangerous and criminal' the acts
Of those fleeing the fallout
    Of our own world-beating bombs and world-bulldozing maps –
Let them not sleep. We sleep with windows wide,
    But to little effect; the heat gives no quarter,
The night too scared to slip inside
    The room and cool us. We lie there, tense, spread-eagled,
As our thoughts rise like notes in the *Nocturnes*
    Into the jellied air
And stall and falter and fall, defeated,
    Useless as a winter prayer.

For Louis, of course, it's winter for real:

In his poem, it's snowing,

The cold is 'unworldly', beyond all appeal,

And though we are promised thunder

No breeze can unstick the shirt from your back,

The exhausting, exhaustive heat a reminder

Of numbers that keep on rising; that crack

Is the crack of an ice shelf calving,

That groan is the jobless rate soaring,

And that intake of breath

Is students watching the politicians

Watch their exam results and tests:

It's not what you know, but what you inherit,

So let ambition, like the very air, congeal,

Set our hopes and notions in aspic

And set the brake to the turning wheel.

What *was* trumps what *is* or what might have been,

And what *was* is a photograph faded to nothing;

Memory's shifting baseline means

We don't even know what it is that we're missing.

We can only know what *we* have lost,

Not what our grandparents knew before us:

A blizzard of birds, cacophony of frogs,

The windscreen spattered with insect corpses,

And I remember dragging my son outside to hear

A cuckoo call, one time; it was a kind of accusation,

Or an alibi or plea, a chance to clear

My name, so that he couldn't say it hadn't happened, ever.

And now I come to them with this box of broken

Toys, saying this was given to me, now it's yours,

This is what you get to build your world with,

And I'm sorry for the scorched earth, the rising waters, the wars,

We assumed someone knew what they were doing,

We couldn't get replacement parts,

We gave the instructions to people
    With money for brains and cheap plastic hearts.
And to add a child to the world is to sign your name
    To the whole world's account, not ever thinking
What debts will accrue and what claims
    Will come due; we are responsible for the politicians
Who filch democracy from under our noses,
    And for their friends the non-executive directors
And the CEOs.
    And in SE26, at last, the weather has broken
And we have had rain.
    And the A-Level students turn on their laptops
To see what the algorithms deign
    To allot them for their lost year's study.
And 'the equation will come out at last,' says Louis,
    But Louis you're naïve.
Someone, not God, wrote that equation,
    It will achieve what they want it to achieve.
And yes the future is always uncertain,
    But it's good to face it with something at your back,
And it's hard to know today what to rely on,
    The line that we held, that was taut, has gone slack.

Written 8–14 August

XXIII

The equation will not come out at last,
    That's not how this equation
With its diverging iterations
    Functions; each version expands on the flaws of the past.
And for sure you can un-do the equation
    But the damage is done all the same,
The fact of its having been written proclaims
    That people rank lower than systems,
And young people lowest of all;
    Set them up to fail, then make of that failure
A ritual trauma:
    And throw their education like a cat against a wall.
Crisis needs crisis management, and this bloody fiasco
    Will ripple out beyond this week,
Stricken universities will creak
    And next year's students suffer also.
The crisis is not the virus but this government
    That seems set on attacking
The public bodies that keep us honest
    And keep us safe – and they *are* bodies, they can be bent
And broken, pushed beyond their limits,
    Harvested for livers, corneas, kidneys, hearts,
And so democracy is stripped for parts,
    And sold on to the highest, unseen, bidder,
And it seems we have forgotten how to shout,
    Or have lost our voices;
Will we get to forgive ourselves our weakness,
    Our failure to act on our justified doubts?

And here, if you want one, is a weakness:

    I envy the poet's foresight:

As he looked out from his autumn night

    And still found grounds for optimism –

And the bastard was right.

    The equation did come out for Britain,

The war was won, and from it we fashioned

    The NHS and the welfare state,

Everything we've grown up to take for granted

    And are losing now to toffs and spivs

Who dress like lawyers and act like thieves

    And know not to waste a good crisis.

So though the crows of plague will flock again,

    And the economy will rise as a zombie

Rises, acting but serving no godly

    Purpose, there will be no war, as there was in Spain,

Then Europe, then the world undivided;

    The war this time will be between

Us and the planet, which obscene

    Senseless struggle can only have one winner, one loser.

And the enemy then was simpler to spot,

    He marched in rank, he wore a devil's

Jacket and spouted fascist venom;

    The enemy today's not so easily got,

His clothes come scented with the promise of riches,

    He speaks in a tongue

That's rung in our ears since we were young.

    Saying: Onwards means upwards, surely,

And good things come to those who meekly wait,

    And if making things is good, then making

Profit's better, no matter if those profits

    End up landing somehow somewhere out of sight.

And this carping seems worse than hopeless,

    It seems to call down defeat

Before the army's even on its feet,

   Before the horse is in its harness.

So Louis, help me: help me find some hope

   In the dark of the August sunshine.

You asked God, if there was one, for courage and vision;

   As well to ask a poet, who must rank as a prelate or pope

In any secular faith worth its trappings and trimmings.

   And, Louis, summer's on the turn,

The midday sun neglects to burn,

   And dusk comes when we're still thinking

Lazy daytime thoughts. And then autumn will come,

   And I'll pass back the baton,

Let you handle your natural season,

   And I'll be there waiting, in March, when you're done.

For as long as there's something vicious looming

   Beyond the horizon, and just as long

As we keep on getting things hopelessly wrong,

   We can keep this thing turning, from poem to poem.

Written 18–21 August

XXIV

Sleep, my notions, sleep, my plans,
　　As this journal slides towards its final pages.
Sleep ambition, sleep, renown,
　　Forgo the early mornings at the laptop –
Or else open the file of the book
　　You were meant to be writing this spring, this summer,
Cautiously, cautiously, wake that up
　　And pray you recognise each other's faces.
And sleep my fellows, sleep my friends,
　　Let go hands, and end all meetings,
When the light of evening ends
　　The night expects you unattended.
And sleep's a sloughing-off of day's cares,
　　We offer ourselves to a deeper knowing,
That knows us better
　　Than we know it, and we hope that it shares
Our days' instinctive hopes and values.
　　And it speaks in dreams that unfold
Like origami flowers
　　That go on unfolding across the world
While we rise unknowing and go about our business;
　　They spread like ripples on a lake
That reach the banks, and are reflected
　　Back, and so the pattern complicates itself, and breaks.
And sleep, the bees in the garden, sleep, the wasps half-drunk
　　On fermenting plums. Sleep, my children,
Who once we sang to sleep from bedroom doorways,
　　But who now slink in late when we're long sunk

In sleep ourselves – sleep, and wake to walk out
    In a landscape not like any in the textbooks:
An earth of fire, flood, and drought,
    Tell me, children, what is wrong with this picture?
And sleep, the ministers and businessmen
    Who drew those pictures
And coloured them so badly in;
    Take away their crayons
And their calculators, take them out to walk the streets
    With that jolly, green-robed giant
Who will show them Ignorance and Want, and so they'll meet
    The workings-out of their precious equations.
And sleep, my sense of perspective; dream
    On your dream of useful poems,
Of the past sleeping while the future wakens,
    Refreshed and invincible, inspired and serene.
Wake, Aleksei Navalny, from your coma,
    Stay awake, Hong Kong, and Belarus,
America, too, is impatient to wake from its fever,
    And if it wakes there's hope for us,
For we follow America like a sleepwalker,
    Or like a toddler aping its parent's nasty tricks,
Mindlessly repeating their way of speaking and shouting
    While what it says is drained of any sense.
And sleep, my poem, sleep, my words,
    A poem is about as much use as a blessing;
Marching songs and lullabies are more effective
    For those who need to cajole and coerce.
Sleep Louis, snug in your hammock, which is woven
    From all the deftest lines you wrote,
The hammock will keep on gently rocking so long as we keep reading,
    And so long as we don't sink the bloody boat.
So sleep to the sound of running water,
    Ripples in a pond, the roar of the sea, a river in spate,

But we do not hear the sound of the sea levels rising,

Disaster always strikes the ear too late.

And the Rubicon is behind us, not in front.

The bomb has already exploded

And future generations will bear the brunt,

While we stagger about, stupefied and overwhelmed.

And yes, there are equations, and equations to spare,

But no 'at last' for them to 'come out' in our lifetime,

Time and the seasons are immune to human despair,

Their 'on' seems to us like a film running backwards:

Tomatoes hang unripened on the vine,

Nasturtiums curl their life into their seedpods,

Swallows gathering on the telephone lines,

As, close and slow, summer is ending in London.

Written 22–28 August

ACKNOWLEDGEMENTS

Thanks go first of all to David Collard, without whose support and encouragement this poem absolutely would not exist in the form you are reading it; then to Michael Hughes, whose superb readings, week by week, helped give the poem its voice. And to the Leapers who responded so positively to the poem as it developed – and especially to the guest readers who made the final full performance such an unforgettable experience: Kevin Boniface, Marie-Elsa Bragg, Season Butler, Susanna Crossman, Kevin Davey, Emma Devlin, Rónán Hession, Amy McCauley, J. O. Morgan, Samuel Skoog, Aea Varfis-van Warmelo and Eley Williams, and to Helen Ottaway and Melanie Pappenheim for the music. Finally, thanks to the Estate of Louis MacNeice for supporting this response to the poet's great work.